D1013315

# Philip Roth at 80

# Philip Roth at 80

## A CELEBRATION

Remarks delivered on the occasion of
Philip Roth's 80th birthday

March 19, 2013
Newark Museum
Newark, NJ

The Library of America
New York • 2014

Published by The Library of America,
14 East 60th Street, New York, NY 10022.
All rights reserved.
No part of this book may be reproduced commercially
by offset-lithographic or equivalent copying devices without
the permission of the publisher.

Visit our website at www.loa.org

Volume compilation copyright © 2014 by
Literary Classics of the United States, Inc.
Contributor's remarks copyright © 2014 to
the individual authors: Jonathan Lethem, Hermione Lee,
Alain Finkielkraut, Claudia Roth Pierpont, Edna O'Brien,
and Philip Roth.

This paper meets the requirements of
ANSI/NISO Z39.48-1992 (Permanence of Paper).

ISBN 978-1-59853-413-9

First Printing

Printed in the United States of America

# Philip Roth at 80

# A Note from the Publisher

This volume has its origin in a program to celebrate Philip Roth's 80th birthday organized by the Philip Roth Society in conjunction with the Newark Preservation and Landmarks Committee. The sequence of the pieces reflects the program order of the live event, which took place on March 19, 2013, in the Newark Museum's Billy Johnson Auditorium in Newark, New Jersey. Some contributors have revised their remarks for this publication; others have chosen to publish their texts as delivered.

The proceeds from the sale of this book will be used to support the mission of The Library of America, a nonprofit organization, publisher of America's best and most significant writing in authoritative new editions, including Philip Roth's collected novels and stories in nine volumes.

# Jonathan Lethem

## The Counter-Roth

### 1.

I'D TAKEN the train out to East Hampton, bringing with me to read only the first volume of John Cowper Powys's *Wolf Solent*. This was an ambiguous mission I was on—I'd been invited to a very nice rich girl's family's summer house, and I'm justified calling her a girl because this was the summer after my first year of college and I was nineteen, a boy of nineteen. We'd been only friends, at college, but might be more, away from college: that was the ambiguous mission. I didn't know what I wanted. On the train I stared out the window, not making it past more than a chapter of the Powys. The girl and her mother picked me up at the station, a five-minute drive there and back, just long enough that by the time we entered the house, through the kitchen, the girl's younger brother was caught in the act of pulling from the broiler two overdone, smouldering lobsters, their red partly blacked. The mother chided him, but affectionately, and insisted the lobsters be dumped immediately in the trash. I thought *I'll eat those*, but no. This was a period in my life where I was persistently being startled, to the point of violation, by the behavior of the wealthy. No reading—not Powys, nor F. Scott Fitzgerald, nor Karl

Marx—could have prepared me to witness such a thing in real life. We ate something other than lobsters. Then I was shown to the guestroom. It was beautifully quiet, with a scattering of books on shelves. An evening seemed to yawn before me—the girl and I would have time to be confused about one another tomorrow, and the next day. Everything was done very graciously in this house, no hurry. Left alone there with ponderous Powys, I reached instead for a book I hadn't known existed: *The Breast*. I'd at that point in my reading life kept a useless partition against Roth, who, thanks to the intimidating aura generated by a paperback copy of *Letting Go* on my mother's shelves, I'd decided was a bestselling writer of grown-up realist novels of a sort that couldn't possibly interest me. Oh judgmental and defended youth! But wait, now I had to consider the claims of the book's dust jacket, that Roth worked in the realm of morbid fantasy, too. The realm of Kafka. This wasn't fair, I thought. Kafka should belong to me. Alone in the East Hampton guestroom, I gobbled *The Breast* in one gulp. That's how it came about, that's how I began taking Roth aboard, the first tiny dose a kind of inoculation to make me ready for the long readerly sickness I still endure. For it is a sickness, most especially for a reader who wants to be a writer, to open oneself to a voice as torrential and encompassing, as demanding and rewarding, as that of Roth. I am therefore here to address you all as my fellow sanitarium inmates, gathered jubilantly and defiantly in the presence of the source of our sickness himself.

## 2.

My situation in the East Hampton summer house was the stuff of Jewish comedy, if I'd had my Jewish antennae up. Had the brother been played by Christopher Walken, I was in a scene from *Annie Hall*. But I not only didn't have my Jewish antennae up, I didn't know I possessed any. By chance, and unlike a majority of Jews, I'd been raised so as not to take being Jewish, or in my case half-Jewish, in any way personally. I'd have to acquire those antennae else-where, by my reading. It took overtly Jewish-American writing—by Bernard Malamud, who'd retired but was still lingering, thrillingly, around at the college the girl and I attended, and Saul Bellow, and yes, sometimes Roth, who is in general overt, and is sometimes, when it serves the cause of the writing, overtly Jewish—to illuminate and make unmistakable what I knew only semi-consciously from the writing of the less-overt, like Nathanael West or Barry Malzberg or Norman Mailer, as well as from sources like Groucho Marx and Abbie Hoffman and my uncle Fred. What was it that was illuminated? That something aggra-vated and torrential in my voice, or perhaps I should call it my attempt at having a voice, was cultural in origin, even if aggravated and torrential frequently in the cause of disput-ing or even denying that point of origin. As Roth points out, the books aren't Jewish because they have Jews in them. The books are Jewish in how they won't shut up or cease contra-dicting themselves, they're Jewish in the way they're sprung both from harangue and from defense against harangue, they're Jewishly ruminative and provocative. Roth once said of Bellow that he closed the distance between Damon

Runyon and Thomas Mann—well, given the generation of readers I'm from, Roth, in turn, closed the distance between Saul Bellow and *Mad Magazine*. That's to say, once I'd gained access to what he had to offer, Roth catalyzed my yearnings to high seriousness with the sense that the contemporary texture of reality demanded not only remorseless interrogation but remorseless caricature and ribbing. Contemporary reality, including perhaps especially the yearning to high seriousness, needed to be serially goosed.

### 3.

Speaking of caricature, I'm aware that having accepted the honor of batting lead-off in this highbrow's lineup I may appear to have lapsed into opening-act schtick—a conflation of potted Rothian syntax and shameless confession. My only defense is that I'm employing tools Roth helped instill in me, tools that may in fact be all I've got: a reliance on the ear, for devising a voice and then following where the voice insists on going, and a helpless inclination to abide with the self—with one's own inclinations and appetites—as a lens for seeing what's willing to be seen, and as a medium for saying what wants to be said. If I'm a poor literary critic, well, you'll get a real one soon enough. If I'm a poor man's Roth, well, you'll get the real Roth soon enough. Call me instead a Counter-Roth. For it is the fate of a Roth, being the rare sort of writer whose major phases sprawl across decades, whose work encompasses and transcends modes of historical fiction, metafiction, memoir, the maximalist (or putters-in), the minimalist (or takers-out), the picaresque and counterfactual, etcetera and so forth—being the sort of writer who in his generosity half blots out the sky of possibility for those who come along after—to generate in his ambitious followers a sort of army of Counter-Roths. I'll say it simply: the one certainty in my generation of writers, not otherwise unified, is that we all have some feeling about Roth. We can't not. Mostly it involves some kind of strongly opinionated, half-aggrieved love.

### 4.

So, another confession: more than ten years after that encounter in East Hampton, I'd become a published novelist invited, for the first time, to a residence at the artist's colony called Yaddo. By this time I'd pursued my Roth obsession to both ends of his bookshelf, as it existed at the time, as I was to continue following it, right up to the present. On my arrival at Yaddo, a fellow writer who helped me to my room at West House mentioned famous personages who'd written masterpieces behind the various windows— Sylvia Plath here, John Cheever there—and then, opening the door to what was to be my residence and studio both, unveiled a circular turret featuring a smooth domed ceiling: "The Breast Room," he announced. I laughed, thinking he referred only to the shape. Then he explained that Roth, inspired by dwelling within the room's contour, wrote *The Breast* there. As with many circumstances in a young writer's life, I was exalted and humbled simultaneously— having been delivered by the Yaddo invitation into what I thought was my maturity, it turned out I was again to suckle at the fount of apprenticeship. Incidentally, if this story isn't true, I don't ever want to find out.

**5.**

Of course I'm beyond my apprenticeship now, and no longer even remotely young. In fact, as a college professor, it's sometimes my duty to counsel other young aspirants navigating an overwhelming encounter with Roth. I'm chagrined to admit that a quite brilliant English major under my care recently quit work on a thesis, on *My Life as a Man*, in despair. With his permission, I quote from the e-mail he sent when, like Nixon, he resigned. "What can I say about Philip Roth that Philip Roth hasn't already said (and denied) (and said again) himself? It's farcical how much *My Life as a Man* exemplifies this tendency. I was being pretty arrogant: if established literary critics cannot produce the kind of scholarship I feel is worthy of Roth's fiction, how could I possibly think myself capable of rising to that challenge, without even reading the work *my* work would supposedly surpass? I feel like a guy taking on the Marines with a single pocketknife. Going forward, here are the options, as I see them: 1) Write as much of a shitty first draft of this chapter as I can and send it to you, then come back to school next semester and write chapters three and four while taking a fuller course load than I did this semester and applying for jobs so that I have somewhere to live and something to do when I graduate. Or, 2) Tolerate the 'Incomplete' on my transcript and take Prof. Dettmar's 'Irony in the Public Sphere' instead. My gut is strongly telling me to choose the latter. I know I fucked up. If I had done the substantial work I should have done earlier this semester, I would either have made this decision at a better time or not made it at all. But here I am. This is okay with me. I'm not going to grad school and I won't be any less fascinated by Philip Roth in letting go of my academic obligation to his books." I quote at length here simply for the pleasure of hearing how the disease has taken hold of the e-mail itself, in its controlled panic bubbles with Rothian verve, even arriving at the key phrase, Letting Go.

## 6.

I only ever made Philip Roth laugh twice, to my knowledge. That's weak recompense for the thousand hilarities Roth's bestowed on me—bitter snorts of recognition, giggles of astonishment at narrative derring-do, sheer earthy guffaws. Of course, I've only ever met him a couple of times, and I'm hoping to add to my score tonight. The first time I made Roth laugh was in recounting a conversation I overheard while on line for a hot dog between innings at Shea Stadium, between two boorish men confessing to one another their preference for a glimpse of tight Spandex even over that of bare skin; I mention this if only for the pleasure of bragging that Roth and I suffer the same fannish encumbrance, for anyone who knows the inside of Shea Stadium has earned whatever joy can be salvaged on the hot dog line. The second time I made Roth laugh is more important to me: we stood together in the late stages of an Upper West Side brunch party, where I dandled my infant son while Roth looked quite reasonably impatient to be elsewhere. In a quiet panic, bobbing up and down to soothe the six-month-old, I found myself monologuing to Roth's increasingly arched eyebrows. Finally, straining for a reference that would interest my hero, I turned the boy's head slightly to the side, displaying the fat curve of his cheek, and said, "It resembles one of those disembodied unshaven cigar-smoking heads in a Philip Guston painting, don't you think?" The juxtaposition of my pink son and the grotesques of Guston, like the earlier juxtaposition of Shea and Spandex, did the trick. And this was another lesson from Roth: In putting across what wants putting across, in seeking a rise from the listener, *do whatever it takes*, grab any advantage, employ even the baby in your arms. I would have *juggled* the baby if it would have helped.

### 7.

To finish, then, with a final confession, according to the Rothian principle of crypto-confessional storytelling: the principle being that though you may in fact hold your cards quite close to your vest, it is best to create the thrilling illusion of having laid oneself generously bare, of having told all. That's simply to say, I don't want to leave you hanging in that East Hampton guestroom. Did I get anywhere with the very nice rich girl? The answer is no. I saw as little action in East Hampton as I'd seen of those lobsters on their voyage from the broiler to the kitchen garbage pail. Less, even, than I'd seen of the lobsters. The only breast I fondled in East Hampton was Roth's.

# Hermione Lee

WHEN I was asked to speak at this birthday celebration, I had the not very good idea of collecting together some 80- or 80-something-year-olds from Philip Roth's books, and of talking about the resilience and energy of old age. I thought of Herman Roth in *Patrimony*, and then I thought—however wonderful that book is, perhaps a talk about a dying 86-year-old father is not the best celebration for a birthday. Then I thought of Murray Ringold, teacher, brother, mentor, at the end of *I Married a Communist*. But when I turned to that magnificent ending I realized that I'd misremembered and that Murray is actually 90. So I was not getting on well.

But re-reading that final conversation between Nathan Zuckerman and Murray Ringold, in which the old English teacher has come to the end of telling Nathan the story of his brother Ira, and is about to leave Nathan alone, with the indispensable stars, my eye snagged on the passage in which Nathan remembers Murray teaching *Macbeth* to his high school class, in about 1948. Murray reads to the class the scene in which Macduff is told of the slaughter of his wife and all his children by Macbeth. The class is sitting very still, here in Newark, waiting for the moment that Macduff will fully understand what has happened. "Outside, a 14 bus is grinding up the Chancellor Avenue hill."

But all the class is listening for is the moment when Macduff will grasp the incomprehensible: "Did you say all? . . . All / At one fell swoop." Malcolm says to him, roughly: "Dispute it like a man." "Then" (Nathan remembers) "the simple line that would assert itself, in Murray Ringold's voice, a hundred times, a thousand times, during the remainder of my life: 'But I must also feel it as a man.'" "Ten syllables," says their teacher, "that's all. Ten syllables, five beats, pentameter . . . eight monosyllables and one word of two syllables, a word as common and ordinary and serviceable as any there is in everyday English . . . and yet, all together, and coming where it does, what power! Simple, simple—and like a hammer."

So this small scene and that plain, simple, powerful line of Shakespeare, which sums up a central theme in Roth's work, settled in my mind as my subject for today. How often, how dramatically, and how usefully, Roth invokes Shakespeare in his comic tragedies of feeling it as a man. How often a performance, on a domestic or internal stage, acts out and embodies the urgent, extreme, inner life of his fictional characters. It's not just Mickey Sabbath in *Sabbath's Theater*, Prospero and Falstaff and Lear and the Fool all rolled into one, who brings Shakespeare into the heart of Roth's fiction.

*Macbeth* is used again for the title of *Exit Ghost* (2007), when Nathan Zuckerman, haunted by the ghost of E. I. Lonoff, makes his own ghostly return and positively final appearance. The title, *Exit Ghost*, faintly echoes a wild Shakespearean riff of fourteen years earlier, in *Operation Shylock*, where a narrator called Philip Roth has to listen to a lecture about Shylock, in Israel, given by Mr. Supposnik, a Tel Aviv rare-book-dealer and member of the Secret Police. In the lecture, entitled "Who I Am," Mr. Supposnik airs his fantasy of being the director of the Supposnik Anti-Semitic Theatre Company, and draws attention to the terrifyingly prophetic stage-direction in *The Merchant of Venice*, "Exit Jew."

Imagining a counterlife as a Shakespearean actor or director is something Roth enjoys. David Kepesh may have turned into a breast, in *The Breast* (1972), but that doesn't stop him doing his imitations of Laurence Olivier as Hamlet or Othello, while he says of his own situation: "This is not tragedy any more than it is farce. It is only life, and I am only human." ("But I must also feel it as a man.")

Simon Axler, the failed actor in *The Humbling*, has had to give up being a classical actor because his performances—of Prospero, of Falstaff, of Macbeth—have become so excruciatingly, ludicrously awful. He can't convince a single person in the audience for a single minute that he is Prospero, Falstaff, or Macbeth. Prospero's lines—"*Our revels now are ended. These are actors, / As I foretold you, were all spirits and / Are melted into air, into thin air*"—go round and round in his mind, so that "the two syllables" of "thin air" come to have "the aura of an obscure indictment." Mind you, his agent Jerry Oppenheim tries to console him, as far as Macbeth is concerned, it's perfectly understandable not to be able to play him—"He's a horrible person for an actor to live with," says Jerry. "I defy anyone to play him and not be warped by the effort."

The nameless "he" of *Everyman* (2006) has his own

Hamlet-like encounter with a grave-digger in a cemetery not so far away from here—a grave-digger who dug his parents' grave, and who is as straightforward and informative with him as Hamlet's grave-digger was. Except Hamlet's grave-digger wasn't black, and he didn't have Thelma to bring him his sandwiches for lunch, "two meat loaf and one baloney."

This riffing on Shakespeare goes back a long way. When Alexander Portnoy is complaining that his mother is telling him all the time to say sorry—why won't he "tell his own mother that he's sorry and will never never do such a thing again, *ever*!"—he says: "Actually what we are playing in that house is some farce version of *King Lear*, with me in the role of Cordelia!"

Why have I chosen to give you these Shakespearean examples from over half-a-century's worth of great novels? I am not quite trying to tell you that Philip Roth is The Bard, and I'm not trying to turn Newark into Stratford-on-Avon or this Newark venue into the Globe Theatre. After all, for one thing, as might already have occurred to you, Shakespeare wasn't Jewish. And for another, Shakespeare didn't live to 80, only to 52—by which time Philip Roth had got as far as *Zuckerman Bound*. My god, think of what Shakespeare might have written if he'd lived as long as Philip Roth!

But I am saying that Roth has Shakespeare deep in his head and that there is something Shakespearean about the way he uses him. David Kepesh, student and professor of literature, has been infatuated since boyhood with the "extreme in literature," and with "imagery and power"—

the power of language to effect "marvelous transforma-
tion." Roth hears and responds in Shakespeare to the
extreme conjunctions of plain, simple, demotic speech and
high rhetoric, the power and audacity of original language,
the bursting out inside tragedy of wild grotesquery and
buffoonery, the leaps of imagination between violence and
pathos, tenderness and savagery, the full-blooded erotics,
the sense of mortality, and the questioning of what it
means to be human.

It would then be nicely poignant to think of Philip
Roth on his eightieth birthday as having burnt through his
phases as Hamlet, Lear, Falstaff and Macbeth, and now, like
Prospero, his book of spells drowned fathoms deep, setting
off homewards, peaceful and philosophical, away from the
magical island of his inventions. But alongside that digni-
fied image of retirement and resignation, I would also
remind you, in Prospero's play, of the raging and dreaming
of Caliban, the violent plots of long-harbored revenge, the
rough demotic comedy of the ordinary sailors, the deception and trickery cunningly magicked up by the airy spirit
of the imagination, and one hell of a tempest.

# Alain Finkielkraut

TO THOSE who, of their own free will or in spite of themselves, overstep all bounds and in so doing are carried away by *hubris*, the Greeks promised the vengeance of *Nemesis*. This purveyor of justice, as the Tragedians teach us, penalizes excess with condign punishment. The Greeks are long gone, but if we are to believe the title of Philip Roth's latest novel and final book, their wisdom still applies.

It is summer of 1944 and America is at war on two fronts. Because he is very short-sighted, Bucky Cantor, a vigorous teacher of physical education in a Newark school, has been declared unfit for military service. He has the muscular build and the athletic prowess of a marine, and he is not a marine. While his best friends are risking their lives on the coasts of Normandy, he is a playground director in Newark, New Jersey. That is exactly what he is ashamed of: the tranquility, the secure life, the obscenity of his privileged situation, until the point when a faceless scourge descends on his little city by-passed by history. That scourge is polio. The epidemic spreads with lightning speed, the youngest being the most vulnerable to it, and this too is a war, "a war of slaughter, ruin, waste, and damnation, war with the ravages of war—war upon the children of Newark."

Albert Camus's novel *The Plague* clearly comes to mind

here, but whereas Camus was writing of a battle and seeking to represent the Resistance, Roth is describing a massacre, and the dazed, powerless state of the innocent victims is discreetly reminiscent of the Holocaust.

Bucky Cantor is disarmed, but he fronts up. For the kids at the playground as well as for the readers, he is "Mr. Cantor," a young man indeed, but a man you can always rely on. And why is that so? Precisely because his family name has precedence over his given name. This Bucky is not a mere individual. He holds himself accountable. He has been raised by a strict, obstinate and loving grandfather. The old man is dead, but he still lives under his eyes. He fulfills the demands made upon him out of respect for his memory. He tries to be worthy of the tenacious grocer. He does his best *not to betray his name*. Known since *Portnoy's Complaint* as the novelist of the *id* and of the raging drives, Philip Roth here, as in *American Pastoral*, pays a magnificent tribute to the *superego*.

Mr. Cantor conceals his own distress. He goes to see the grief-ridden parents. He also soothes the vindictive frenzy of those desperately seeking a scapegoat. However, after having initially refused to desert Newark to join Marcia—the girl with whom he is madly in love—at a summer camp far from the epidemic, he yields when she accepts his engagement proposal. But this return to nature proves illusory. There is no idyllic way out. Like Oedipus who, with every move that he makes to escape the oracle, is in fact accomplishing it, Bucky Cantor sees the illness he thought he was fleeing arise in Indian Hill, and he realizes he is himself carrying the virus. He survives but remains disabled and breaks with Marcia to free her from the burden he would represent. She begs him not to do so, but he remains adamant. He condemns himself thereby to a dreary loneliness. Those things we learn from the narrator of *Nemesis*, who for a long time remains discreet and almost invisible. Arnie Mesnikoff meets Mr. Cantor some thirty years after the event. He was one of the playground children. He contracted the illness and also bears its scars, but he is married and reasonably happy.

As in a novella by Henry James, the terrible revelation of the missed opportunity emerges from this encounter. This difference in life-stories unveils Mr. Cantor's other severe pathology: *the pathology of explanation*. Everything has to make sense. Nothing can happen without a reason. At the beginning of the epidemic, he accused the Creator of all things and hence of the polio virus. Then, though not reconciled with heaven, he turned his metaphysical rage onto himself: he was the transgressor, he brought the virus, he contaminated the camp and that made him a perfect culprit for his ferocious superego. There was no place in Mr. Cantor's mind and sensibility for contingency. "The devout individual," writes the French philosopher Clément Rosset, "is first and foremost, a person incapable of confronting the non-necessary." Even though he denigrated God, Mr. Cantor was, to his own misfortune, a *devout*. Instead of marrying Marcia, as he wished, he pleaded guilty and may have ruined both their lives.

It is his refusal of the tragic that plunges Mr. Cantor into tragedy. And the *nemesis* that strikes him is not the answer "to the *hubris* of will or desire" but the response to the hubristic need to find a cause, to know why. Mr. Cantor is "a martyr of the why."

There are very few people as scrupulous as Bucky Cantor in our postmodern world of given names. But one way or another, we are all the more inclined to fall into what Chesterton would have called the *madness of reason*, that we confuse it with intelligence. Philip Roth is not content, therefore, simply to describe its ravages. He refutes it by chronicling in *Nemesis* an epidemic that did not take place, but threatened to do so, bringing with it the panic fear of catching the virus and being confined to an iron lung. Inspired, as in *The Plot Against America*, by what another great novelist—Robert Musil—ironically terms "the principles of insufficient reason," Roth dissipates the illusion of necessity and restores to the past its fragile, random character. What did happen might have happened differently. And this difference is worth exploring: nothing is true in *Nemesis*. But out of the total fiction invented by Philip Roth is born the unforgettable truth of a very decent man crushed by his sense of honor and his inability to accept the element of luck and absurdity involved in all things human.

# Claudia Roth Pierpont

THERE are many things that Philip Roth is well known for writing about. In the introduction to my new book about his work, I made a list of some of the broader subjects he has addressed over the years, and these include: Jews in America, Jews in history, sex and love and sex without love, the need to find meaning in one's life, the need to change one's life, parents and children, the trap of self and the trap of conscience, American ideals, the American betrayal of American ideals, the upheavals of the sixties, the Nixon presidency, the Clinton era, Israel, the mysteries of identity, the human body in its beauty, the human body in its corrupting illness, the ravages of old age, the coming of death, the power and failings of memory. No wonder it took him thirty-one books to get it all in.

But tonight, I want to look at subjects that are less often discussed. In fact, I'd like to look at three of these subjects: two just rather briefly, because they come to mind when I think about the little explored Roth, and because they lead to a third subject—the women in his fiction—that I'd like to talk about at greater length.

The first thing I'd like to mention is the music in his books. I mean this in two ways: first, the music that he actually writes about, music as a subject. Even in this one area, there's a tremendous range: from the Mozart that inspires Alexander Portnoy's stolid flaxen-haired girlfriend, whom he calls The Pilgrim, to her first bold act of fellatio— it's the Clarinet Quintet, a particular favorite of Roth's—to, at the other end of his career, the Artie Shaw arrangement of "The Man I Love," with trumpet by Roy Eldridge, that Faunia Farley dances to, naked, for Coleman Silk, in *The Human Stain*. While Faunia is dancing, she tells Silk that even though he's seventy-one (and she's thirty-four) he isn't old enough for her, that she needs a guy "who's had all the love-shit kicked out of him." She tells him, "I need a man at least a hundred. Do you have a friend in a wheelchair you can introduce me to? Wheelchairs are okay—I can dance and push."

Of course, in Roth's work, there's also music that doesn't accompany sex and love and human connection but that replaces these things, or comes as close as anything can to replacing them: the piano practice that David Kepesh buries himself in after Consuela leaves him, in *The Dying Animal*; or the music that the old and sexually incapacitated Nathan Zuckerman, in *The Human Stain*, listens to every single evening, when he's all alone on his mountaintop retreat in the Berkshires—music that doesn't interrupt the silence, he says, but that seems to him like "the silence coming true." And when the pianist Yefim Bronfman walks onto the stage at Tanglewood, also in *The Human Stain*, and begins to play Prokofiev's Second Piano Concerto, it's about as powerful an experience for Zuckerman as sex was to Roth's libidinous hero Mickey Sabbath, in *Sabbath's Theater*, and has the same ultimate if illusory power. Zuckerman thinks: "Our own lives now seem inextinguishable. Nobody is dying, *nobody*—not if Bronfman has anything to say about it!"

But then there's the other kind of music, too—the music that Roth creates himself, the music of his language. To best suggest this music I should read one of his great descriptive catalogues, like Mickey Sabbath's inventory of Debbie Cowan's underwear drawer, or Swede Levov's survey of the land around his house in *American Pastoral*, or Sabbath's memories of his childhood on the Jersey shore:

> There was sand and ocean, horizon and sky, daytime and nighttime—the light, the dark, the tide, the stars, the boats, the sun, the mists, the gulls. There were the jetties, the piers, the boardwalk, the booming, silent, limitless sea. Where he grew up they had the Atlantic. You could touch with your toes where America began. . . .

That's just a taste of it. It's hard not to want to sing these lines.

But then I'd also like to mention a second if admittedly more marginal subject that never gets discussed: silverware. Knives and especially forks, and the uses to which people put them. Mrs. Portnoy standing over little Alex with a bread knife, making certain that he eats—the knife, he remembers years later, had "little sawlike teeth." And the fork that is an even more dangerous weapon in the final scene of *American Pastoral*, when a drunken guest at the Levovs' Labor Day party tries to stab Swede Levov's father, Lou Levov, in the eye with one. I used to think that Dickens had the greatest fork in fiction, in *Bleak House*, when Esther finally gets to her bedroom in Mrs Jellyby's chaotic house, manages to close the door without crushing the little fingers

of the many Jellyby children in its hinges, looks in relief
toward the window and sees that the curtain is held in place
with—a fork. Roth had a trial run for his own great fork
scene when, in *Operation Shylock*, Moishe Pipik lunges at
Jinx Possesski with a fork, and stabs the back of the hand
she has just used to cover her eye. (I expect that all of this
will be detailed someday in a dissertation, "Flatware in
Dickens and Roth.") Fortunately, in *American Pastoral*, the
drunken woman—her name is Jesse Orcutt—who attempts
to stab Swede Levov's father in the eye also misses. What
has happened is that the supremely well-meaning if relent-
less Lou Levov has pushed aside the unhappy woman's glass
of whiskey, replaced it with a glass of milk, and is patiently
feeding her a piece of pie, forkful by forkful, when she
announces that she will feed herself—and instead, goes
straight for his eye, missing by about an inch.

And then another woman at the party starts to laugh.
Her laughter is the last sound that we hear in the book.
"Not bad for somebody as drunk as this babe is," she says,
leaving *American Pastoral* to end in a mixture of tragedy
and slapstick that is one of the most distinctive aspects of
Roth's genius.

Everybody who's read *American Pastoral* must remember the scene, but you may not remember the laughing
woman's name. She's a minor character, and her name is
Marcia Umanoff. She's a left-wing college professor, a
Manhattan intellectual, a smart if maybe too opinionated
person who is adored by her husband but whom neither
Swede nor Dawn Levov can stand. And what she's laughing
about, Roth tells us, in this novel about the upheavals of the

sixties—about the political, social and moral upheavals of those years, about the domestic effects of the Vietnam War—what she's laughing about is "how far the rampant disorder has spread"; what she's enjoying is "the assailability, the frailty, the enfeeblement of supposedly robust things."

It was when thinking about Marcia Umanoff and Jesse Orcutt and Faunia Farley and Dawn Levov and Debbie Cowan's mother, Michelle, that I realized that there's a subject in Roth's work that's been given less consideration than music or even silverware. And that is the quality of his female characters, in all their comedy, tragedy, complexity, and humanity.

There are no generalizations to be made about Roth's women, any more than about his men. They are strong, vulnerable, smart, not so smart, wise or shallow people with their own aims and their own psyches. They struggle, as the men do, with the restrictions and permissions of their times: with their, and our, history. There is no way to discuss them—to give a sense of their range—except as individuals. So I'd like to talk about a number of the women that Philip Roth has added to the world, female characters I think about and live with, the way one lives with all the characters that mean a lot to one in books, as in life.

*Sabbath's Theater* is a very cheerfully dirty-minded book about grief and death. By the time that it was published, in 1995, readers were already familiar with the idea in Roth's work of sex as freedom—of sex as a perfectly wonderful thing in itself, of course, but also of sex as a protest against the most pressing social and ethical and even political constraints, ranging from the teenage agonies of Alex Portnoy to the tyranny of Communist Prague under the Soviet heel in "The Prague Orgy." But *Sabbath's Theater* elevates sex into a protest against the grave itself. And its hero, Mickey Sabbath, protests quite a lot. Yet he has met his match in a short, dark-haired, middle-aged Croatian woman, an émigré to America—a bit on the plump side—named Drenka Balich, a woman whose contempt for rules surpasses even Sabbath's.

Drenka is funny, warm, hard-working, highly sexed and entirely original. She is also an old-fashioned, loving mother—an attribute as important to her makeup as any of the others. After she takes five hundred dollars from Sabbath in a little sex game they play, in which she pretends to be his whore, she uses the money to buy a set of power tools for her grown son, who happens to be a police officer. She has already bought herself a radio scanner that monitors police signals, so she can keep track of her son when he's on duty all night. This is serious mothering. But the thrill for Sabbath is in the contradiction, in having found what he calls "a respectable woman who was enough of a warrior to challenge his audacity with hers."

What Sabbath means by this is that Drenka—who is a good wife, too, in her way, if to someone other than Mickey Sabbath—is an enthusiastic and gifted adulteress. Yet, in the relationship between Sabbath and Drenka, it isn't only the sex, or the daring in the sex, or the defiance of convention in the sex, that matters. That's the easy stuff at this point in history. The truly surprising aspect of their affair is not its every-which-way sex but—so much harder to bring off—the depth and innocence of their love.

How many great love affairs have there been in recent fiction? This one lasts thirteen years. And then, at fifty-two, Drenka gets sick and dies, sending Sabbath on a downward spiral—he decides to try to commit suicide—and starting the novel on its course. Like *Lolita*, *Sabbath's Theater* is a retrospective account of an illicit passion—illicit because both Sabbath and Drenka are married and are dedicatedly promiscuous. But, in this case, the woman is anything but a nymphet. In fact, middle-aged Drenka is anything but the conventionally lusted-after heroine of contemporary culture, as Sabbath makes clear when, after thirteen years, he ponders her undiminished physical appeal:

> It was supposed to be otherwise, with the musculature everywhere losing its firmness, but even where her skin had gone papery at the low point of her neckline, even that palm-size diamond of minutely crosshatched flesh intensified not merely her enduring allure but his tender feeling for her as well. He was now six short years from seventy: what had him grasping at the broadening buttocks as though the tattooist Time had ornamented neither of them with its comical festoonery was his knowing inescapably that the game was just about over.

The great gift that Roth bestows on Drenka is not beauty but an absolute, good-natured freedom, which is based in strength and radiates joy. She is described (by Sabbath) as "plainly ecstatic to be living on earth," and as "a piece of human sunlight" by her doting if clueless husband. She's an intoxicating earth mother, absolved of sentimentality by raunchy sex and weight around the hips.

It is easy to enjoy her, and impossible not to weep along with Sabbath at her death bed. It's a stretch to call Mickey Sabbath a hero, but Drenka Balich is a worthy descendant of the great adulteresses of European literature.

And then there is the way that Drenka speaks. Roth's heroes are known for their sexual animation. One of his heroes, the literature professor David Kepesh, was once mysteriously transformed into a 5' 11", one hundred and fifty-five pound breast, for no apparent reason except that he taught Kafka and Gogol with a little too much conviction. But it's important to note that Roth's heroes are also, in fact, and increasingly throughout his career, voice men, suckers for a woman's wit and words. Even Alexander Portnoy finally rejects his flaxen-haired beauty because he can't bear what he calls her "cutesy-wootsy boarding school argot."

As for Drenka, Sabbath calls the effect of her words and her voice "phonetic seduction." He relishes her "juicy" accent and, even more, her émigré's knack for turning American clichés into little verbal artworks, on the order of: "it takes two to tangle," "I've got to get quacking," and "a bottomless piss." To Sabbath, the lack of cliché in the way she speaks is a sign of the lack of cliché in the way she thinks and lives. Linguistic torture, on the other hand, is inflicted by the college girl who tells him that she feels "empowered" by knowing him, employing what Sabbath calls "that language which they all used and which made him want to cut their heads off."

In *The Counterlife*, Roth's most constant and cerebral protagonist, Nathan Zuckerman, falls in love with an Englishwoman named Maria Freshfield, a "deliciously civilized" woman, as Nathan puts it, who is able to quote John Donne with ease, and whose most intoxicating trait is the fluency, command, and sheer beauty of her speech— "those gently inflected English ups and downs," again, as Nathan says. In fact, Nathan utters barely a word about his lover's face or hair—we never learn if she is dark or fair— nor has he anything to say about her legs or her breasts. It turns out that Nathan Zuckerman is willing to put his life on the line for Maria Freshfield because of what he calls "a finely calibrated relative clause."

We know what Faunia Farley looks like in *The Human Stain*. She isn't beautiful, either. She's tall and blond but drawn and thin-lipped, with an unsettling hardness to her gaze. But she was a beautiful child. After growing up in a well-to-do Boston home, she has become who she is—a janitor at a college in the Berkshires, "exiled from the entitlement that should have been hers"—after being sexually abused by her stepfather from early childhood and running away, at fourteen. At twenty, she married a dairy farmer, a Vietnam vet who started beating her when the farm went broke. She had two children who died—Faunia believes the deaths were her fault, and she is probably right—and she has survived a couple of suicide attempts. But if Faunia is broken, she remains very much alive. Roth gives her a stoic calm that is not the same as strength but that serves well enough in its place. At thirty-four, she is still, in some ways, "the kid who mistrusts everyone, sees the con in everyone, and yet is protected against nothing, whose capacity to hold on unintimidated is enormous, and yet whose purchase on life is minute."

The person describing Faunia is her lover, Coleman Silk, the hero of *The Human Stain*, who is not only much older than Faunia but is a retired professor at the college where she works as a janitor. Coleman is able to tell Faunia the secrets of his own past, to tell them for the first time in his life—those of you who have read the book know that this has to do with his family and his race—because, despite the accusations of people who see him as merely exploiting a woman of lower status, Faunia is for him "the unlikely intimate with whom he shares no less a spiritual than a physical union," and "more to him like a comrade-in-arms than anyone else on earth." Faunia has been through hell and keeps on going. And, as Coleman Silk says, "that is when you love somebody, when you see them being game in the face of the worst."

It's Faunia who comes up with the phrase that gives the novel its title—the human stain—and Faunia who introduces the philosophy that lies behind it. When Faunia needs to secure her sense of calm she drives to the local Audubon preserve, where she communes with a caged, misfit crow, a bird that was hand-raised by humans and can't be freed without being attacked by other crows, because he doesn't sound like them: he learned to caw by imitating the schoolchildren who stood outside his cage imitating a crow. As Faunia sees it, "That's what comes of hanging around all his life with people like us. The human stain." Faunia says this straightforwardly, without any sense of condemnation: "*That's how it is.*" In Philip Roth's scale of values, this clear-eyed acceptance of reality is a serious virtue. Nathan Zuckerman admires Faunia for acknowledging what other people pretend not to see—and, elaborating her thoughts into a near theology of impurity, he accounts for a great deal about the lives of all of Roth's characters, male and female:

> We leave a stain, we leave a trail, we leave our imprint. Impurity, cruelty, abuse, error, excrement, semen— there's no other way to be here. Nothing to do with disobedience. Nothing to do with grace or salvation or redemption. It's in everyone. Indwelling. Inherent. Defining. The stain that is there before its mark. Without the sign it is there. The stain so intrinsic it doesn't require a mark. The stain that *precedes* disobedience, that *encompasses* disobedience and perplexes all explanation and understanding. It's why all the cleansing is a joke. A barbaric joke at that. The fantasy of purity is appalling.

Drenka Balich and Faunia Farley and Maria Freshfield are major characters in their respective books, and there are other major figures worth talking about: Lucy Nelson in Roth's 1965 novel *When She Was Good*, who is literally driven mad by the restrictions and expectations of her life in a small Midwestern town in the fifties; the young Radcliffe student Brenda Patimkin of *Goodbye Columbus*, clever and daring as, aided by reading Mary McCarthy, she edges toward the sixties; the passionately literary Amy Bellette, whom we get to know both in her mysterious youth, in *The Ghost Writer*, and much later, in *Exit Ghost*— the books were written nearly thirty years apart—where Roth returns to Amy at age seventy, her body riddled with cancer but the literary devotion that gives her life purpose wholly undiminished. And there is the other side of Amy, Roth's most uncanny heroine, the ghost of *The Ghost Writer*, Anne Frank—a latter-day, surviving Anne Frank, a heartbreaking young woman living on the thinnest edge between history and imagination.

Yet just as fascinating as these major figures, in many ways, are the women Roth has created as quick pencil sketches, so to speak, women conjured out of a bare minimum of pages—like Marcia Umanoff, like Michelle Cowan—who are nevertheless important to the story and to the reader, who are remarkably knowable and real.

Michelle Cowan, in *Sabbath's Theater*, is a minor character with major impact, a portrait of the successful middle-aged woman as a secret, Bovaryesque malcontent and sexual outlaw. She's married to a good-hearted man, she has a successful career and a daughter at Brown. And yet, as Sabbath sees it, "There is something in her that is always threatening to undo it all, the warmth, the comfort, the whole wonderful eiderdown that is their privileged position." Because Michelle is the only person in the book who, after Drenka's death, shares Sabbath's painfully con-flated sense of sex and loss. She's fifty-five years old, she's menopausal, and she feels that "*everything* is racing off at a tremendous speed." She has hot flashes, which Sabbath sees not merely in a sympathetic light but in an exalted one: "Dipped, she is, in the very fire of fleeting time." (Or, less poetically, "It's no fun burning on a pyre at dinner.") It's no surprise that Mickey Sabbath—steadfastly dirty old man, descendent of Falstaff—sees nobility in Michelle's persistent adultery, in her refusal to go gently into unsexed darkness.

But he convinces the reader, too, that Michelle, like Drenka, is somehow a morally dedicated adulteress, a magnificent Molly Bloom refusing to let anything go:

> Must everything be behind her? No! No! The ruthless
> lyricism of Michelle's soliloquy: and no I said no I will No.

To suggest the range of these rapid portraits, I'd like to mention Anna Ziad, in *Operation Shylock*: an intense, migraine-afflicted, psychologically complex Palestinian woman, and an unforgettable sketch of female pragmatism and anguished motherhood. Anna has moved from Boston to the West Bank with her teenage son and her husband, who was a professor of literature before he took up the permanently embittering, nearly deranging struggle to regain his family's old house and land in Jerusalem. And Anna is choking over what she considers to be her husband's destructive loyalties. "Why aren't you loyal," she demands, "to your *intellect*? Why aren't you loyal to *literature*?" She values her son's future—which she sees being destroyed— far above what she calls the "childish, stupid ethnic mythologies" that she sees on both sides, and she argues:

> Isn't it "life" when you read books and listen to music
> and choose your friends because of their qualities and
> not because they share your roots? Roots! A concept for
> *cavemen* to live by!

I was so moved and persuaded by Anna that I once asked Roth if there had been a real-life model for her. He said no, that he had simply tried, and I quote him, "to reverse the stereotype, a process that usually leads you toward reality." A couple of years ago I happened to write an article about contemporary Arabic fiction, books that have been appearing increasingly in English translation, and I found that the most lauded modern Arabic novel of the Palestinian struggle, the Lebanese writer Elias Khoury's *Gate of the Sun*, which was based on hundreds of oral histories, features a heroine with absolutely no biographical similarities with Anna Ziad but with absolutely similar pragmatic and protective strengths.

There are many more women in many more trying, testing situations. There's Jinx Possesski's harrowing experience as a cancer nurse, in *Operation Shylock*, and Delphine Roux's uneasy bargain with contemporary academia in *The Human Stain*. There is Ernestine Silk, also in *The Human Stain*, a strong and self-assured African American schoolteacher who has to come to terms with why her brother deserted his family and his race. And there's young Philip Roth's mother, Bess Roth, in *The Plot Against America*, a stalwart heroine in the face of her government's turn to fascism, who uses the simplest domestic tools at hand—a telephone, a box of Rice Krispies—to comfort a terrified and suddenly orphaned child halfway across the country.

Kate O'Hearn, the long-deceived wife of the philandering poet George O'Hearn, in *The Dying Animal*, gets hardly more than a paragraph and a single spoken line to establish her own brand of clear-eyed wisdom. Kate is an imposing, more-than-middle-aged, white-haired woman, "attractively roundish, wry, resilient, radiating a kind of stubborn heartiness." She ends up standing at her profligate husband's deathbed, in the presence of their grown

children, when, semi-paralyzed after a stroke, he calls her
to him, begins to kiss her passionately, and then begins to
fumble with his one good hand at the buttons of her blouse.
Kate kisses him back, and then, at the prompting of her
daughter—everyone in the room is intensely moved—
begins to help him with the rest: first the buttons on her
sleeves, then down the blouse's front. George is trying to
undo her bra when he suddenly falls back on his pillows,
not yet dead but with his final act on earth cut short. It's a
grand, touching, almost Victorian scene of the dying profligate redeemed. Immediately afterward, Kate walks a friend
who's been at the bedside down the driveway to his car—a
friend who tells her excitedly how glad he was to have witnessed such a scene—and, deflating the drama with a
weary smile, she says, "I wonder who it is he thought I
was." Talk about clear-eyed acceptance of reality . . .

And lest you think that all of these women are resigned
to adultery, or glory in it, there is Phoebe in *Everyman*,
who catches her husband betraying her after many years of
marriage and throws him out. Roth says that he particu-
larly enjoyed writing Phoebe's furious, parting speech:

> Oh, why go on—all these episodes are so well known.
> . . . The man loses the passion for the marriage and he
> cannot live without. The wife is pragmatic. The wife is
> realistic. Yes, passion is gone, she's older and not what
> she was, but to her it's enough to have the physical affec-
> tion, just being there with him in the bed, she holding
> him, he holding her. The physical affection, the tender-
> ness, the comradery, the closeness. . . . But he cannot

accept that. Because he is a man who *cannot live with-out*. Well, you're going to live without now, mister. You're going to live without plenty. You're going to find out what living without is all about!

And he does.

In closing, I want to say that I did once complain to Roth about one of his female characters—about Jamie, in *Exit Ghost*. She's thirty years old, she's rich, she's sexy, she's a writer, she has a curtain of dark hair and she wears a thousand dollar cashmere cardigan over a little lingerie top and, frankly, I think she made me a little jealous. As I said, these characters are very real to me. After I read the book, I said to Roth, somewhat sniffily, "She's kind of perfect, isn't she?" Actually, Jamie isn't perfect, she has her share of problems, but I was feeling sniffy. And he gave me the perfect answer, an answer that shows how very real all these characters are to him, too. He said to me, "You should hear what *she* says about *you*."

# Edna O'Brien

THERE IS a poem by Yeats, written in the last years of his life, called "Beautiful Lofty Things," in which he summons remarkable people he knew, revolutionaries, poets, his father, Lady Gregory, the beautiful Maud Gonne, and concludes with the line "All the Olympians; a thing never known again." There is a tendency to celebrate dead Olympians, but today we're here for one who is alive and who, until recently, used to think that eighty was a house number and not a birthday. I met Philip Roth in the late seventies, when he came to dinner at my house in London. It was not auspicious. There he sat, lean, watchful and scorchingly handsome. In those days I was a gushing and eager cook. Suddenly, coming out of his reverie, he said, "Do you do the soup and the soufflés in between writing your books?" I smarted somewhat. It was in an Irish accent and a not very convincing Irish accent. We met a few more times when I found that the innate reserve had slipped somewhat.

But things transpire and one day there was a pounding on my door in Carlyle Square and there was Mr. Roth in a lather of rage and self-righteousness. He had done a version of *The Cherry Orchard*, in which Claire Bloom was to appear at Chichester Theatre, and rehearsals were not going to his liking. He was not being listened to, he was not consulted, he was relegated and felt himself to be a minion. He was also hyperventilating. I lived opposite a square and thought some fresh air might lessen the intemperance, but out there, his fury magnified. He threw himself on the grass, the damp grass I should add, and railed against the injustices and stupidities of mankind. I urged him to get up, in case some roving reporter might chance to be going by and we would be subjected to a headline—"Irish Woman Rescues Famous Author."

I was invited to the opening night at Chichester, which went well, and next day Claire, Philip and I walked on the Sussex Downs and came into a field of bleating lambs. "Let's get out of here, it's like a maternity ward" Philip said, whereupon we climbed into a field, where somewhat determined-looking bullocks began to stalk towards us. With no wish to be an instant heroic boy scout, Philip suggested that we retreat, which we did. A country walk with Philip does not have the zeal of Dorothy and William Wordsworth, where every nuance of nature has to be noted and jotted down. On quite a different walk many years later, in Connecticut, we were on a narrow path by a riverbank, not a soul in sight, when around a corner there emerged a benighted figure in a hooded jacket and Philip said "Hey, it's Salman Rushdie"—it being only a couple of days after Rushdie's fatwa had been pronounced. I mention these somewhat idle occasions to give some idea of his prodigious energy and zest, no moment passed without a blizzard of joke, anecdote, rascally ribbing, a mind spiralling almost, though never fully, out of control. Sometimes it occurred to me that to live at that altitude must be lonely, rather like the trapeze artist, up there, with nobody else in his orbit. There is of course the other side, the listener, the one who listens and empathizes with what he hears. He is gladiatorial if writers he admires are being demeaned and no more tellingly than when he felt that towards his friend Saul Bellow and acted with what Dean Swift calls fierce indignation. When I had some prolonged roasting from critics, he said, "I don't like what they're doing to you" and took it upon himself to persuade Mike Levitas of *The New York Times Book Review* to arrange a conversation interview. Just as we sat down in front of the tape recorder at my kitchen table in London, he nudged me and said "Hey, I don't want you to come out smarter or more intelligent than me" and so I didn't.

We are in New York in a restaurant on the West Side, where they serve lobster. He decides I would like lobster. It entails having a bib put over my front because of the spatters when tearing out the flesh from the claws and I think I won't have lobster, as it's all too surgical and demanding, he thinks differently. There is a small demur and I yield to having the lobster as the bib is tied around my neck. Oh yes, we discuss literature, but without the commodious baggage. He liked what Joyce once said to an acolyte, "Don't talk to me about literature, talk to me about turnips." When he decides to, Philip is flawless in his appraisal of the written word, always getting to the pith, whether it's Hans Castorp in the snows and the throes of unrequited love, or Simon Sebag Montefiore's life of Hitler or Stalin, one feels he has read with utter concentration and will only speak of a work that he has thought deeply about.

Ask him, what, in two words, is so great about his beloved
Faulkner and he replies "Dark Knowledge." Ask him what
is great about Kafka and with sudden effervescence he
dilates for a moment to describe a walk with Mr. Singer on
86th Street, with Mr. Singer pointing nostalgically to windows of apartments, where he enjoyed romantic trysts with
numerous women who would be at home in those pre-
feminist days and who then in parenthesis described Kafka
as "a wallflower." So what does Philip have to say about
Kafka? No two words would convey the enormity of his
admiration, the extent of his debt. On another occasion, he
arrives at a restaurant, flings down a piece of folded paper
and says "Sign that or else." He then takes the piece of
paper back and all through the evening asks if I am going
to comply. All this with the menace of a mobster. I never
knew what was written on the folded page, whether it was a
living will, a marriage proposal or the telephone number of
his favorite baseball hero. Every moment charged and
stoked with suspense.

In Connecticut he was different, untypically docile, in
from his studio, like a working man who had done his eight
hour shift and left it to others to provide the verbal calis-
thenics. Inwardly he was with his work, the way writers
always are. But domestic bliss, as such, came to an end and
with the purposefulness of a Samurai, he entered the prolonged spate of solitude, the bare desk, what Robert Lowell
called "the poet's guillotine." Breaking loose from worship-
ping family or friends, from marriage and from what he
once called "the moral propriety" of his earlier work, he
wrote his great books, books with the ebullience he likes,

the precision he insists on, the occasional blasphemy and a greater gravity, the artist's chronicle of a world, our world "gone berserk." But these books did not come without a price and without crisis, so that there were pills, potions, the services of psychiatrists, a discipline, which in a moment of exasperation he described "as the crudest weapon since the leech pot." Friendships were either postponed, mistrusted or severed. I went once during that hermetic time and I too felt ostracized. It was as if I had betrayed him in some unknowing way and the door was metaphorically shut. But we survived it.

It has been assumed that we had a love affair and I have to confess that we didn't. However, a student has pointed out to me that perhaps I am the prototype for Caesara O'Shea in his novel *Zuckerman Unbound*. Caesara, keeper of the screens, inviting lilt, is descended from a niece of Noah who, to escape the flood, sailed in some rudimentary vessel to Ireland, a country that has its own floods. There, her ancestors built a hut and one had even cut turf for Mary Magdalene. Caesara, with her charm and inherited blarney, escapes her woebegone surroundings to be embraced in the Hollywood pantheon, but her time is running out. She recites Yeats "mistily," is an admirer of Richard Ellmann, and has had a burst appendix. Some of these qualities might pertain, but not all. While ogling Zuckerman in New York, she is the creature of Fidel Castro and is bound for her appointment in Havana. I did attend an eight hour marathon in Havana listening to Fidel, where no erotic musings bestirred me, simply the fear that I would expire from the heat and the exhaustion. What I do like about the Caesara connection is that both she and Zuckerman are "intensity afflicted." It is thought that Philip doesn't like women, well maybe he doesn't, but he certainly has loved a few. One has only to read his books to recognize that like every man he suffers from temptation, is over-vulnerable to female beauty, prone to the mania of uncertainty and longing, confessing to loves that have almost destroyed him and to a rabid faithlessness—"As the flower is gnawed by frost, so every human heart is gnawed by faithlessness."

People who know that I know him often ask me about Philip, not without a certain prurience. Well, he's paralyzingly funny, morally rigorous, he is not a Bohemian, he dishes out his own cornflakes in the morning and is the most consistent tuning fork of the written word. He loves good or great writing and by association, good or great writers, even the ones he can't abide to be with. He is at the top table of the literary establishment, but he is not of it, too wild, too aesthetically honed and too honest. To hear him list the literary gentlemen and gentlewomen, Vaselined from head to toe in hypocrisy as they greet their peers in the hope of advancement, is to be treated to a modern Restoration comedy. He is a frugal man, but also capable of real and subtle generosity. The defining influences on him are his parents, his father Herman, the hardworking Jew in a Gentile insurance colossus, and the mother's faithful husbandry. Each week she put two dollars into a jug, so that the family could go to Jersey Shore for the annual hol. His book *Patrimony*, though raw and searing, is infused with tenderness, in which ultimately, he the son, with a child's conscience, is at the mercy of the father, the Moses-like figure, sitting in judgment on what the son does and on what he writes. I asked him once what his relationship was with his mother and this is what he said—"Soon as I had a mouth before the age of three she was my slave." Did she love him? "Love me—she adored me, I was too adorable for words." With his first substantial check he bought her a present of Japanese seed pearls, which she kept, as she would a relic, in the silk drawstring sachet in which they had come.

So, friends, this is the tip of the iceberg, I can only give you a glimpse of the complexity of the man that is Philip Roth, feared and revered, plagiarized, envied, hermit and jester, lover and hater, by his own admission foolish and yet fiercely formidable, too adorable for words, a true friend and undoubtedly one of Yeats's Olympians.

# Philip Roth

TEMPTING AS it is, I will not bury you tonight beneath a ton of stories about my happy childhood in the Weequahic section of this city or about my emotional affinity to nearly every commonplace, unpoetic thing that was the Newark of my day. There is no good reason for an eighty-year-old man to regret that things were once different or to bore people with a pathetic fondness for carrying on about how everything back then was otherwise.

The Weequahic section is a twenty-minute bus ride from this spot. I know because we made school trips by bus to the museum to look at the famous jewelry collection, many of the pieces Newark-made, when I was a pupil at Chancellor Avenue Elementary School from 1938 to 1946.

But I'll say no more about Chancellor Avenue School or about how, when I was a pupil there, there were only eight teams in the National League and eight in the American or about how we used to painstakingly pick the silver foil clean from the empty cigarette packs we found crumpled up in the gutter and roll them into a substantial ball of foil that we carried with our school books to school for the war effort.

Nor will I tell you about the most thrilling day of my young American life, August 14, 1945, when, after three and a half years of our living in a mobilized country at war on two enormous fronts—each at the opposite rim of the Eastern Hemisphere—Japan, our last enemy, surrendered. Or about the most thrilling night of my young American life when the Democrat Truman upset the Republican Dewey in 1948. Or about the longest, saddest day of my young American life, the spring day in April 1945, less than four weeks before the war against Nazi Germany ended in Europe, when Roosevelt, four times elected, president of the United States from the day I was born, died suddenly of a cerebral hemorrhage at the age of sixty-three. Our family seething in sadness. Our *country* seething in sadness.

Between December 1941 and August 1945, an American child didn't just live at home, in the neighborhood, and at school. If the child was at all attentive and curious, he or she also lived within the ethos of a tragic catastrophe that was global. The terrifying symbol of its tragic nature was the plain little gold-star flag, about half the size of our car's license plate, that hung in the front window where a son or a father or a husband of the household had been killed in action. The mother of that family became known as "a Gold Star Mother." There were two such flags in the windows of flats along our Newark street, and it was difficult for most kids to pass those windows on the way to school in their usual childish state of school-going levity.

I wondered back then what it could possibly be like for a child having to tiptoe into one of those houses as a member of the grieving family, sobbing with everyone over dinner, falling stricken into one's bed at night, awakening horrified every morning, mute with grief in the home that lay behind the drawn blackout shades and that gold-star flag, in rooms still harrowingly rich with the mementos and memories of the dear one only recently robbed of the rest of his life. How would the bereft creature who was one-self ever again be a child? I wondered what it would be like never again to know delight.

Some forty years later, when I came to write *Sabbath's Theater*, I found out for myself by imagining the anguish of the grieving Sabbaths of Bradley Beach, New Jersey.

I will not test your patience tonight with stories about the Osborne Terrace Library, a small branch of the main Newark library a mile or so from my house, and of how I bicycled there as a boy every two weeks to borrow books. I carried the books home, half a dozen at a time, in the basket of my bike. But I've told that story already and prob-ably, you are thinking, in more than one book. Nobody needs to hear any more about my bicycle basket.

In my defense, however, I should insert here that remembering objects as mundane as a bicycle basket was a not insignificant part of my vocation. The deal worked out for me as a novelist was that I should continuously rum-mage around in memory for thousands and thousands of just such things. Unlikely as it may seem, a passion for local specificity—the expansive engagement, something close to fascination, with a seemingly familiar, even innocuous, object like a lady's kid glove or a butcher shop chicken or a gold-star flag or a Hamilton wristwatch, according to Poppa Everyman the Elizabeth, New Jersey, jeweler, "the best watch this country ever produced, the premier Ameri-can-made watch, bar none."

I was saying that this passion for specificity, for the

hypnotic materiality of the world one is in, is all but at the heart of the task to which every American novelist has been enjoined since Herman Melville and his whale and Mark Twain and his river: to discover the most arresting, evocative verbal depiction for every last American thing. Without strong representation of the thing—animate or inanimate—without the crucial representation of what is real, there is nothing. Its concreteness, its unabashed focus on all the particulars, a fervor for the singular and a profound aversion to generalities is fiction's lifeblood. It is from a scrupulous fidelity to the blizzard of specific data that is a personal life, it is from the force of its uncompromising particularity, from its *physicalness*, that the realistic novel, the insatiable realistic novel with its multitude of realities, derives its ruthless intimacy.

Enjoined to this verbal task, I must add, until about three years back, when I for one awoke one fine morning with a smile on my face, understanding that miraculously, seemingly in my sleep, I had at long last eluded my lifelong master: the stringent exigencies of literature.

I will not speak about the park, Olmsted's vast and beautiful Weequahic Park, our wooded, hilly countryside, our skating pond, our fishing hole, our necking parlor, our pick-up place, where Portnoy's uncle Hymie parked his car to pay cold cash to the Polish janitor's shiksa daughter Alice to stay away from his son Heshie.

Or about the dirt playing field, a hundred and fifty yards long, some sixty yards wide, a big field just down Summit Avenue from my house. Steam-shovels had gouged it out of the Chancellor Avenue hill in the 1930s. "The field" was what everyone called it, the field where, in *Nemesis*, Bucky Cantor throws the javelin. "Running with the javelin aloft, stretching his throwing arm back behind his body, bringing the throwing arm through to release the javelin high over his shoulder—and releasing it then like an explosion."

I am finished with that stuff too. I've described my last javelin throw and my last stamp album and my last glove factory and my last jewelry store and my last breast and my last butcher shop and my last family crisis and my last unconscionable betrayal and my last brain tumor of the kind that killed my father.

I don't want to describe the blade of the auger that you use for ice-fishing or a boy ecstatically bodysurfing at the Jersey Shore or Newark, this city, going up in flames or the U.S. under President Charles Lindbergh or Prague under the totalitarian boot of the Soviet Union or a Jewish superpatriot's diatribe in a West Bank settlement or a Christmas carol service seated beside an anti-Semitic sister-in-law in a London church or the moral unreadiness of the parents of a terrorist daughter or what Shakespeare called "the fangs of malice."

I don't want to describe, spadeful by spadeful, how a grave is dug or how it is filled back up to the brim. I don't want to describe another death or even just the simple drama of the daily pleasure of living the human comedy. I don't wish any longer to contemplate in fiction the destructive, the blighted, the bruised, the assailable, the accused, their accusers, or even those who are whole, sane, and beautifully intact and who accept life bravely and joyfully.

I won't tell you tonight about the prize fights at Laurel

Garden. You saw a snippet of a championship fight, usually a penultimate knockdown followed by the crushing knock-out, in the newsreels on Saturday afternoons at the Roo-sevelt Theater. But you only witnessed the damage being inflicted first-hand—the brute force up close—at Newark's Laurel Garden. The sporting arena was located on Spring-field Avenue not that far from this museum.

The war. The school. The park. The field. The museum. The library. The fights. All of which over the years inspired in me, when I was working at my best, what I once described elsewhere as "that lubricious sensation that is fluency."

For a treat, my father took my older brother and me to the fights when we were kids. This wasn't New York and Madison Square Garden in its heyday, it was Newark and Laurel Garden during the war and so half the fighters were bums. My brother and I would bet a nickel on each fight—one of us taking the black guy and the other the white guy or if both fighters were of the same race we bet the light trunks versus the dark trunks. On a bad night I could blow my weekly twenty-five cent allowance at the fights.

But fight night at Laurel Garden provided a sublime experience for a ten-year-old boy. It was practically a spiri-tual phenomenon. For me it had the synagogue beat by a mile. Mischievous, masculine joys! You could be asphyxi-ated by merely one gulp of what passed for air inside Laurel Garden. Grown men, in gruff, indignant voices that sounded comically musical to my ears, would roar abusive encouragement at the fighters. The coarse Newark libretto for an *opera buffa*.

And that, by the way, was how I found out half the

fighters were bums. I would never have known on my own. But the wise guys, the tough guys, the roughnecks and hoodlums seated upstairs in the gallery—collectively smoking themselves to death—told the whole smelly arena as much. "You bum! You bum you!" A boy's first encounter with the thrilling profane.

I won't tell you about seeing Jackie Robinson in 1946, the year before he broke into the lily-white big leagues, with the Brooklyn Dodgers, as baseball's first black player. He was with the Brooklyn farm club then, the Montreal Royals. They were playing against our triple-A Yankee minor league farm club, the Newark Bears, at Ruppert Stadium here in the Fifth Ward, the working-class neighborhood more evocatively known both as Down Neck and the Ironbound.

At a quarter a ticket on weekdays, it was just us kids, boys still blessedly ignorant of eros whose greatest lust was no less for the subtleties than for the individual heroism of the game of baseball. It was just us boys and the drunks scattered thinly about in the bleachers. Most of the drunks didn't bother anyone but slept the afternoon away whimpering and snoring in the summer sun.

But there was one of them, I remember, an inspired one, who would rouse himself every inning or so and, looking groggily around, try to figure out where he was. And then, no matter what was going on in the game—about which he had no idea—he would stand up and, swaying on wobbly legs, enigmatically holler from between his hands, "Walk eem, walk eem—he's a bad man!"

But you surely didn't come over to Newark to sit here

all night listening to this stuff. Professor Finkielkraut tells me that the Greek rhetorical term for this stuff—for saying you are not going to talk about something and then, for a doubtful ironic effect, talking about it—is either "paralipsis" or "prolepsis." Best then to take a less classical approach from here on out, one easier for even a friendly audience to bear, even if it doesn't camouflage one's emotions quite so well.

### 2.

Before I read from my 1995 novel, *Sabbath's Theater*, allow me to say something about the book and its protagonist.

*Sabbath's Theater* takes as its epigraph a line of the aged Prospero's in act five of *The Tempest*, Prospero's concession that as inexpungible a truth as there is—the irksome law of cessation—has come to permeate his brain.

"Every third thought," says Prospero, "shall be my grave."

I could have called the book *Death and the Art of Dying*. It is a book in which breakdown is rampant, suicide is rampant, hatred is rampant, lust is rampant. Where disobedience is rampant. Where death is rampant.

Mickey Sabbath doesn't live with his back turned to death the way that normal people like us do. No one could have concurred more heartily with the judgment of Franz Kafka than would Sabbath, when Kafka wrote, "The meaning of life is that it stops."

To meet the dead, to be reunited with them, is never far from Sabbath's mind. The closer he gets to the dead—to *his* dead—the stronger the geyser of tormented feeling and the further he moves from the wild and antagonistic performance that is his life. The book is a savage journey with the dead into his own raw wound.

His book is death-haunted—there is Sabbath's great grief about the death of others and a great gaiety about his own. There is leaping with delight, there is also leaping with despair. Sabbath learns to mistrust life when his adored older brother is killed in World War II. It is Morty's death that determines how Sabbath will live. The death of Morty sets the gold standard for grief.

Through the blow of death Sabbath is edified way ahead of his time by the crises that are born of contingency. He is transformed utterly at the age of fifteen by the unimaginable made gruesomely real, when everything essential to life disappears in a blink.

Alas, in this novel, the corpses aren't hidden under the floor upon which the living dance through life. Here the corpses get to dance too. No death goes undescribed, and no loss either. Everybody who enters here, everybody, is wedded to death and nobody escapes grieving. There is loss, death, dying, decay, grief—and laughter! Ungovernable laughter! Pursued by death and followed everywhere by laughter.

This Sabbath is a jokester like Hamlet, who winks at the genre of tragedy by cracking jokes as Sabbath winks at the genre of comedy by planning suicide.

Yet where love is great and loss real—as with his brother, his mother, his father, and Drenka, the mistress he visits nightly while she pitilessly wastes away on her deathbed—there the guile disappears. Then even Sabbath, corpulent, cunning, imprudent, arthritic, defeated, unpardonable Mickey Sabbath, loathsome and clad like a freak though he is, hurled perpetually from levity to gravity, from repugnance to melancholia, from mania to buffoonery, out of sympathy with the august moral sentiments and the laudable ideologies of communal accord, a kiln of antagonism, and like so much of flawed humanity, unable ever to tear free of himself, this very same Sabbath is carried off by extremes of misery.

Such depths as Sabbath evinces lie in his polarities. What's clinically denoted by the word "bi-polarity" is something puny compared to what's brandished by Sabbath. Imagine, rather, a multitudinous intensity of polarities, polarities piled shamelessly upon polarities to comprise not a company of players but this single existence, this theater of one.

Unlike Swede Levov in my subsequent novel, *American Pastoral*, Sabbath is anything but the perfect external man. His is, rather, the instinctual turbulence of the man beneath the man: the unmanageable man, the unexonerated man— better, the refractory man: refractory meaning "resistant to treatment or cure," refractory meaning "capable of enduring high temperatures." Refractory not as a pathology but as a human position. The refractory man being the one who will not join.

His refractory way of living—unable and unwilling to hide anything and, with his raging, satirizing nature, mocking everything, living beyond the limits of discretion and taste and blaspheming against the decent—this refractory way of living is his uniquely Sabbathian response to a place where nothing keeps its promise and everything is perish-

able. His refractory way of living, a life of unalterable con-
tention, is the best preparation he knows of for death. In
his incompatibility he finds his truth.

### 3.

To commemorate my having been generously granted
sufficient time and enough good health to have finished
thirty-one books, I want to read to you some pages that I
like as well as any pages I've ever written. And, after having
recently concluded over half a century struggling with
writing, I'm far from liking all of the pages I've written.

Here is Sabbath at a cemetery at the Jersey Shore
searching alone for the graves of his grandparents, his parents, and Morty, the brother whose twin-engine B-25J was
shot down as he piloted a routine bombing run over the
Japanese-occupied Philippines on December 13, 1944. It is
fifty years later yet Mickey Sabbath, now 64, searches still
for the irreplaceable brother. Loss governs his world.

From *Sabbath's Theater*, the bottom of page 363 to the
middle of 370.

> Getting to the old graves, to the burial ground
> established in the early days by the original seashore
> Jews, he gave the funeral in progress a wide berth and
> was careful to steer clear of the watchdogs when he
> passed the little prayer house. These dogs had not yet
> been made conversant with the common courtesies, let
> alone the ancient taboos that obtain in a Jewish ceme-
> tery. Jews guarded by dogs? Historically very, very
> wrong. His alternative was to be buried bucolically on
> Battle Mountain as close to his late mistress, Drenka, as

he could get. This had occurred to him long before today. But whom would he talk to up there? He had never found a goy yet who could talk fast enough for him. And there they'd be slower than usual. He would have to swallow the insult of the dogs. No cemetery is going to be perfect.

After ten minutes of rambling about in the drizzle, searching for his grandparents' graves, he saw that only if he traveled methodically up and down, reading every headstone from one end of each row to the other, could he hope to locate Clara and Mordecai Sabbath. Footstone inscriptions he could ignore—they mostly said "At Rest"—but the hundreds upon hundreds of headstones required his concentration, an immersion in them so complete that there would be nothing inside him but these names. He had to shrug off how these people would have disliked him and how many of them he would have despised, had to forget about the people they had been alive. Because you are no longer insufferable if you are dead. He had to drink in the dead, down to the dregs. They were buried, after all, not that far under the crust of the earth.

Our beloved mother Minnie. Our beloved husband and father Sidney. Beloved mother and grandmother Frieda. Beloved husband and father Jacob. Beloved husband, father, and grandfather Samuel. Beloved husband and father Joseph. Beloved mother Sarah. Beloved wife Rebecca. Beloved husband and father Benjamin. Beloved mother and grandmother Tessa. Beloved mother and grandmother Sophie. Beloved mother

Bertha. Beloved husband Hyman. Beloved husband Morris. Beloved wife and mother Rebecca. Our beloved daughter and sister Hannah Sarah. Our dear father Marcus. On and on and on.

Nobody beloved gets out alive. Our son and brother Nathan. Our dear father Edward. In memory of my beloved husband and our dear father Lewis. And on mine, beloved what? Just that: Beloved What. David Schwartz, beloved son and brother, died in service of his country 1894–1918. In memory of Gertie, a true wife and loyal friend. Our son, nineteen years old, 1903–1922. No name, merely "Our son."

And here we are. Sabbath. Clara Sabbath 1872–1941. Mordecai Sabbath 1871–1923. There they are. Simple stone. And a pebble on top. Who'd come to visit? Mort, did you visit Grandma? Dad? Who cares? Who's left? What's in there? The box isn't even in there. You were said to be headstrong, Mordecai, bad temper, big joker . . . though even you couldn't make a joke like this. Nobody could. Better than this they don't come. And Grandma. Your name, the name also of your occupation. A matter-of-fact person. Everything about you— your stature, those dresses, your silence—said, "I am not indispensable."

No contradictions, no temptations, though you were inordinately fond of corn on the cob. Mother hated having to watch you eat it. The worst of the summer for her. It made her "nauseous," she said. I loved to watch. Otherwise you two got along. Probably keeping quiet was the key, letting her run things her way. Openly partial to Morty, Grandpa Mordecai's namesake, but who could blame you? You didn't live to see everything shatter. Lucky. Nothing big about you, Grandma, but nothing small either. I'll still take you just as you were. A kind and gentle soul who persevered. Life could have marked you up a lot worse. Born over there in the tiny town of Bilkamin, died here at Pitkin Memorial.

Have I left anything out? Yes. You used to love to clean the fish for us when Morty and I came home at night from surf casting. Mostly we came home with nothing, but the triumph of walking home from the beach with a couple of big blues in the bucket! You'd clean them in the kitchen. Fillet knife right at the opening, probably the anus, slit it straight up the center till you got behind the gills, and then (I liked watching this part best) you would just put your hand in and grab all the good stuff and throw it away. Then you scaled. Working against the scales and somehow without getting them all over the place. It used to take me fifteen minutes to clean it and half an hour to clean up after. The whole *thing* took you ten minutes. Mom even let you cook it. Never cut off the head and the tail. Baked it whole. Baked bluefish, fresh corn, fresh tomatoes, big Jersey tomatoes. Grandma's meal.

Yes, it was something down on the beach at dusk with Mort. Used to talk to the other men. Childhood and its terrific markers. From about eight to thirteen, the fundamental ballast that we have. It's either right or it's wrong. Mine was right. The original ballast, an attachment to those who were nearby when we were learning what feeling was all about. A good thing to be able to contemplate for a final time—certain high points, certain human high points.

Hanging out with the man next door and his sons. Meeting and talking in the yard. Down on the beach, fishing with Mort. Rich times. Morty used to talk to the other men, the fishermen. Did it so easily. To me everything he did was so authoritative. One guy in brown pants and a short-sleeve white shirt and with a cigar always in his mouth used to tell us he didn't give a shit about catching fish (which was lucky, since he rarely pulled in more than a sand shark)—he told us kids, "The chief pleasure of fishing is getting out of the house. Gettin' away from women."

We always laughed, but for Morty and me the bite was the thrill. With a blue you get a big hit. The rod jolts in your hand. Everything jolts. Morty was my teacher fishing. "When a striper takes the bait," he told me, "it'll head out. If you stop the line from paying out it'll snap. So you just have to let it out. With a blue, after the hit, you can just reel it in, but not with a striper. A blue is big and tough, but a striper will fight ya." Getting blowfish off the hook was a problem for everybody but Mort—spines and quills didn't bother him. The other thing that wasn't much fun to catch was rays. Do you remember when I was eight how I wound up in the hospital, Grandma? I was out on the jetty and I caught a huge ray and it bit me and I just passed out. Beautiful, undulating swimmers but predatory sons of bitches, very mean with their sharp teeth. Ominous. Looks like a flat shark. Morty had to holler for help, and a guy came and they carried me up to the guy's car and rushed me to Pitkin.

Whenever we went out fishing, you couldn't wait for us to get back so you could clean the catch. Used to catch shiners. Weighed less than a pound. You'd fry four or five of them in a pan. Very bony but great. Watching you eat a shiner was a lot of fun, too, for everyone but Mother. What else did we bring you to clean? Fluke, flounder, when we fished Shark River inlet. Weakfish. That's about it.

When Morty joined the Air Corps, the night before he left we went down to the beach with our rods for an hour. Never got into the gear as kids. Just fished. Rod, hooks, sinkers, line, sometimes lures, mostly bait, mostly squid. That was it. Heavy-duty tackle. Big barbed hook. Never cleaned the rod. Once a summer splashed some water on it. Keep the same rig on the whole time. Just change the sinkers and the bait if we wanted to fish on the bottom.

We went down to the beach to fish for an hour. Everybody in the house was crying because Morty was going to war the next day. You were already here, Grandma. You were gone. So I'll tell you what happened. October 10, 1942. He'd hung around through September because he wanted to see me bar mitzvahed, wanted to be there. The eleventh of October he went to Perth Amboy to enlist.

The last of the fishing off the jetties and the beach. By the middle, the end of October, the fish disappear. I'd ask Morty—when he was first teaching me off the jetties with a small rod and reel, one made for fresh water— "Where do the fish go to?" "Nobody knows," he said. "Nobody knows where the fish go. Once they go out to sea, who knows where they go to? What do you think, people follow them around? That's the mystery of fishing. Nobody knows where they are."

We went down to the end of the street that evening and down the stairs and onto the beach. It was just about dark. Morty could throw a rig a hundred and fifty feet even in the days before spin casting. Used the open-faced reels. Just a spool with a handle on it. Rods much stiffer then, much less adroit reel and a stiffer rod. Torture to cast for a kid. In the beginning I was always snarling the line. Spent most of the time getting it straightened out. But eventually I got it. Morty said he was going to miss going out fishing with me. He'd taken me down to the beach to say so long to me without the family carrying on around us.

"Standing out here," he told me, "the sea air, the quiet, the sound of the waves, your toes in the sand, the idea that there are all those things out there that are about to bite your bait. That thrill of something being out there. You don't know what it is, you don't know how big it is. You don't even know if you'll ever see it." And he never did see it, nor, of course, did he get what you get when you're older, which is something that mocks your opening yourself up to these simple things, something that is formless and overwhelming and that probably is dread. No, he got killed instead.

And that's the news, Grandma. The great generational kick of standing down on the beach in the dusk with your older brother. You sleep in the same room, you get very close. He took me with him everywhere. One summer when he was about twelve he got a job selling bananas door-to-door. There was a man in Belmar who sold only bananas, and he hired Morty and Morty hired me, age 7. The job was to go along the streets hollering, "Bananas, twenty-five cents a bunch!" What a great job. I still sometimes dream about that job. You got paid to shout "Bananas!"

On Thursdays and Fridays after school let out for the day, he went to pluck chickens for the kosher butcher, Feldman. A farmer from Lakewood used to call on Feldman and sell him chickens. Morty would take me along to help him. I liked the worst part best: spreading the Vaseline all the way up your arms to stymie the lice. The chickens were infested with lice. It made me feel like a little big shot at eight or nine not to be afraid of those horrible swarming lice, to be, like Mort, utterly contemptuous of them and just pluck Feldman's chickens.

And he used to protect me from the Syrian Jews. Kids used to dance on the sidewalk in the summertime outside Mike and Lou's. Jitterbug to the jukebox music. I doubt you ever saw that, Grandma. When Morty was working at Mike and Lou's one summer he'd bring home his apron and Mom would wash it for him for the next night. It would be stained yellow from the mustard and red from the relish. The mustard came right with him

into our room when he came into our room at night.
Smelled like mustard, sauerkraut, and hot dogs. Mike
and Lou's had good hot dogs. Grilled.

The Syrian guys, the Syrian Jews, used to dance outside Mike and Lou's on the sidewalk, used to dance by
themselves together like sailors. They had a little kind of
Damascus mambo they did, very explosive steps. All
related they were, clannish, and with very dark skin. The
Syrian kids who joined our card games played a ferocious blackjack. Their fathers were in buttons, thread,
fabrics then. Used to hear Dad's crony, the upholsterer
from Neptune, talking about them when the men played
poker in our kitchen on Friday nights. "Money is their
god. Toughest people in the world to do business with.
They'll cheat you as soon as you turn around."

Some of these Syrian kids made an impression. One
of them, one of the Gindi brothers, would come up to
you and take a swing at you for no reason, come up and
kill you and just look at you and walk away. I used to be
hypnotized by his sister. I was twelve. She and I were in
the same class. A little, hairy fireplug. Huge eyebrows.
I couldn't get over her dark skin. She told Gindi something that I said, so once he started to rough me up.
I was deathly afraid of him. I'm still afraid of him. I
should never have looked at her, let alone said anything
to her. But the dark skin got me going. Always has.

He started to rough me up right in front of Mike
and Lou's, and Morty came outside in his mustard-
stained apron and told Gindi, "Stay away from him."
And Gindi said, "You gonna make me?" And Morty

said, "Yes." And Gindi took one shot at him and opened
up Morty's whole nose. Isaac Gindi. His form of narcis-
sism never enchanted me. Sixteen stitches. Those
Syrians lived in another time zone. They were always
whispering among themselves. But I was twelve, inside
my pants things were beginning to reverberate, and
I could not keep my eyes off his hairy sister. Sonia.
Sonia was her name. Sonia had another brother, as I
recall, Maurice, who was not human either.

But then came the war. I was thirteen, Morty was
eighteen. Here's a kid who never went away in his life,
except maybe for a track meet. Never out of Monmouth
County. Every day of his life he returned home. Endlessness renewed every day. And the next morning he goes
off to die. But then, death is endlessness par excellence,
is it not? Wouldn't you agree? Well, for whatever it is
worth, before I move on: I have never once eaten corn
on the cob without pleasurably recalling the devouring
frenzy of you and your dentures and the repugnance
this ignited in my mother. It taught me about more than
mother-in-laws and daughter-in-laws; it taught me
everything. This model grandmother, and Mother had
all she could do not to throw you out into the street.
And my mother was not unkind—you know that. But
what affords the one with happiness affords the other
with disgust. The interplay, the ridiculous interplay,
enough to kill all and everyone.

Beloved wife and mother Fannie. Beloved wife and
mother Hannah. Beloved husband and father Jack. It
goes on, the names as proximate to them as we can get.

The names one never has to struggle to recall. Our beloved mother Rose. Our beloved father Harry. Our beloved husband, father, and grandfather Meyer. People. All people.

In the earth turned up where Leah Goldman, another devoted wife, mother, and grandmother, had just been united with one of her family, a beloved one as yet unidentified, Sabbath found pebbles to place on the stones of his mother, his father, and Morty.

Here I am.

# Notes on the Contributors

**Jonathan Lethem** is the author of *The Fortress of Solitude* and eight other novels; his ninth, *Dissident Gardens*, appeared in 2013. His books have been translated into over thirty languages. He edited the three-volume Library of America edition of Philip K. Dick's fiction. He lives with his family in Maine and Los Angeles.

**Hermione Lee** is President of Wolfson College, Oxford, a Fellow of the Royal Society of Literature, a Fellow of the British Academy, and member of the American Academy of Arts and Sciences. She is the author of biographies of Virginia Woolf and Edith Wharton and of books on Willa Cather, Elizabeth Bowen, and Philip Roth. Her most recent book, a life of Penelope Fitzgerald, was published in 2013.

**Alain Finkielkraut** was born in 1945. He teaches philosophy at the École Polytechnique in Paris and is a member of the Académie Française. Among his books are *Le juif imaginaire* (*The Imaginary Jew*), *La défaite de la penseé* (*The Defeat of the Mind*), *La sagesse de l'amour* (*The Wisdom of Love*), and two books of literary essays: *Un coeur intelligent* (*The Intelligent Heart*, with a chapter on *The Human Stain*) and *Et si l'amour durait* (*And If Love Lasted*, with a chapter on *The Professor of Desire*).

**Claudia Roth Pierpont** is a staff writer at *The New Yorker*, where she has worked for more than twenty years. She is the author of *Passionate Minds: Women Rewriting the World*, a collection of essays about women writers, and of *Roth Unbound: A Writer and His Books*, published by Farrar, Straus and Giroux in 2013.

**Edna O'Brien** has written over twenty works of fiction along with biographies of James Joyce and Lord Byron. She is the recipient of many awards, including the Irish Pen Lifetime Achievement Award, the American National Art's Gold Medal, and the Ulysses Medal. Born and raised in the west of Ireland, she has lived in London for many years.

# The Library of America Philip Roth Edition

**Novels & Stories 1959–1962**
*Goodbye, Columbus and Five Short Stories* • *Letting Go*

**Novels 1967–1972**
*When She Was Good* • *Portnoy's Complaint* • *Our Gang* •
*The Breast*

**Novels 1973–1977**
*The Great American Novel* • *My Life as a Man* •
*The Professor of Desire*

**Zuckerman Bound: A Trilogy & Epilogue 1979–1985**
*The Ghost Writer* • *Zuckerman Unbound* • *The Anatomy Lesson* •
*The Prague Orgy* • Previously unpublished television screenplay
for *The Prague Orgy*

**Novels & Other Narratives 1986–1991**
*The Counterlife* • *The Facts* • *Deception* • *Patrimony*

**Novels 1993–1995**
*Operation Shylock* • *Sabbath's Theater*

**The American Trilogy 1997–2000**
*American Pastoral* • *I Married a Communist* • *The Human Stain*

**Novels 2001–2007**
*The Dying Animal* • *The Plot Against America* • *Exit Ghost*

**Nemeses**
*Everyman* • *Indignation* • *The Humbling* • *Nemesis*

For more information, visit: **www.loa.org/roth**

This book is set in 11 point Minion Pro, a digital typeface designed by Robert Slimbach in 1990 for Adobe Systems and inspired by Renaissance-era fonts. The name comes from the traditional nomenclature for type sizes, the smallest of which was diamond, followed by pearl, agate, nonpareil, minion, brevier, bourgeois, long primer, small pica, pica, etc.

The text paper is acid-free Sebago Antique, manufactured by the Lindenmeyr Paper Company; it meets the requirements for permanence established by the American National Standards Institute. The binding material is Rainbow Ultima 7, which features a water-based acrylic undercoat and clear acrylic top coat.

Design and composition by
The Library of America, New York, New York.

Printing and smyth-sewn binding by
Courier Corporation, Westford, Massachusetts.